# secrets to building a thriving business

## Your guide to turning your business into a success

By

# Arnold c Hoffman

# Table of contents

## Introduction

Unveiling the secrets to building a thriving business unveils a journey laden with strategic decisions, resilience, and visionary foresight. This guide is a treasure trove of insights, unveiling the crucial elements essential to not just establishing a business, but nurturing its growth and ensuring sustainable success in an ever-evolving marketplace. Delving deep into the intricacies of entrepreneurship, this exploration navigates through the strategic maneuvers, innovative approaches, and indispensable lessons that lay the foundation for transforming a business idea into a flourishing venture. From cultivating a resilient mindset to crafting effective strategies, fostering customer relationships, and navigating challenges with resilience, this guide serves as a beacon for entrepreneurs seeking to unlock the elusive secrets behind creating and sustaining a thriving business in today's competitive landscape.

## Chapter 1

Strategic planning serves as the compass guiding businesses toward success in an ever-evolving landscape. It's the cornerstone of establishing a clear roadmap, defining objectives, and charting the course for achieving long-term goals. This process involves a systematic analysis of internal strengths, weaknesses, external opportunities, and threats to formulate actionable strategies. By aligning resources, setting priorities, and adapting to changing market dynamics, strategic planning enables businesses to seize opportunities, mitigate risks, and stay agile in pursuit of sustained growth and competitive advantage.

It empowers organizations to make informed decisions, optimize operations, innovate, and navigate uncertainties with resilience, ensuring they remain on a trajectory towards achieving their envisioned success.

Strategic planning is also the crucial process for achieving business success. It involves setting clear objectives, evaluating the current market landscape, and developing strategies to accomplish those goals. Here are some key steps in strategic planning:

**1. Assessing the current situation:** A comprehensive analysis of the organization's strengths, weaknesses, opportunities, and threats (SWOT analysis) helps identify areas that need improvement and potential advantages to leverage.

**2. Defining the mission, vision, and values:** Clearly defining the purpose and direction of the business helps align decisions, actions, and strategies with the overall objectives.

**3. Setting goals and objectives:** Specific, measurable, achievable, relevant, and time-bound (SMART) goals are established to provide a roadmap for success. These goals should align with the organization's mission and vision.

## 4. Conducting market research:

Understanding customers, competitors, and market trends is vital for making informed decisions and identifying growth opportunities. This research helps businesses stay ahead of the competition and adapt to changing consumer demands.

## 5. Developing strategies: Based on the

analysis and research findings, strategies are devised to achieve the defined objectives. These strategies may include market penetration, product development, market expansion, diversification, or innovation.

**6. Implementation and execution:** The formulated strategies are put into action through a well-structured implementation plan. This plan defines responsibilities, timelines, resources, and milestones.

**7. Monitoring and evaluation:** Regularly reviewing the progress allows businesses to identify any deviations from the plan and make necessary adjustments. Evaluating outcomes helps measure success and understand areas for improvement.

**8. Adapting to change:** The business environment is dynamic, so it's essential to continuously monitor market trends, customer preferences, and industry developments. Adaptability and agility are crucial for long-term success.

Overall, strategic planning is an ongoing process that requires collaboration and involvement from different stakeholders within the organization. It helps steer the company in the right direction, identify growth opportunities, and navigate challenges that come along the way.

**Chapter 2**

Building a business from scratch is a transformative journey filled with challenges, innovation, and perseverance. It begins with a vision, an idea that ignites the spark of entrepreneurship. This journey involves meticulous planning, resource allocation, and a relentless pursuit of turning that idea into a reality. Starting from ground zero demands a blend of determination, adaptability, and a willingness to embrace the unknown.

Entrepreneurs often start by conducting market research, identifying their target audience, and crafting a unique value proposition. From there, creating a solid business plan becomes imperative, outlining the mission, strategies, and operational framework. Securing funding, whether through personal savings, investors, or loans, is often a crucial step in kickstarting the business.

Building a team of dedicated individuals and assembling the right talent is vital. As the business takes shape, branding, marketing, and customer acquisition strategies play pivotal roles in establishing a presence in the market.

Navigating challenges, learning from failures, and iterating on strategies become the norm. Flexibility and adaptability are key as entrepreneurs constantly refine their approaches based on market feedback and changing dynamics.

Ultimately, building a business from scratch requires resilience, creativity, and a relentless pursuit of innovation. It's a journey that demands commitment, dedication, and the ability to turn obstacles into opportunities, ultimately leading to the creation of a sustainable and successful venture.

It also requires careful planning, diligent execution, and resilience in the face of challenges. It involves several key steps, including market research, developing a solid business plan, securing financing, building a team, marketing and promoting your products or services, and continuously adapting to the changing business landscape. Let's dive deeper into each of these steps to provide you with a more comprehensive answer:

**1. Market Research:** Before starting a business, it's crucial to identify and understand your target market, consumer needs, and potential competition. Conducting thorough market research will help you identify your niche, determine the demand for your products or services, and develop effective marketing strategies.

**2. Business Plan:** A well-crafted business plan serves as a roadmap for your business. It outlines your goals, target market, product/service offerings, marketing strategies, financial projections, and more. A solid business plan helps you stay focused and provides guidance to potential investors or lenders.

**3. Financing:** Securing the necessary funding is a critical aspect of building a business. You can explore various funding options such as self-financing, loans, grants, crowdfunding, or seeking investors. It's crucial to create a financial plan that details startup costs, ongoing expenses, and realistic revenue projections.

**4. Building a Team:** As your business grows, assembling a dedicated and skilled team becomes crucial. Define the roles and responsibilities you need to fill, and hire individuals who align with your vision and values. Building a strong team will help you achieve your business goals and drive success.

**5. Marketing and Promotion:** Effective marketing strategies are essential for attracting customers and establishing a strong brand presence. Utilize both online and offline channels such as social media, advertising, public relations, content marketing, and networking to reach your target audience and differentiate yourself from competitors.

**6. Adaptability:** The business landscape is constantly evolving, so it's important to remain adaptable and open to change. Regularly evaluate market trends, customer preferences, and industry developments to fine-tune your strategies and offer innovative solutions.

## Chapter 3

Creating a successful business model involves several key steps and considerations:

**1. Identify a Problem or Opportunity:** Start by understanding a problem or identifying an opportunity in the market that your business can address or capitalize on. Conduct market research to validate the need or demand for your product or service.

**2. Value Proposition:** Clearly define what value your business offers to customers. What makes your product or service unique or better than existing options? Your value proposition should address the pain points of your target audience.

**3. Target Audience:** Identify and understand your target audience or customer segment.

Know their preferences, behavior, and needs to tailor your offerings effectively.

**4. Revenue Streams:** Determine how your business will generate revenue. Explore various monetization strategies such as sales of products, subscriptions, advertising, or licensing.

**5. Cost Structure:** Understand the costs associated with running your business. This includes expenses related to production, marketing, operations, staffing, technology, and more. Ensure that your revenue covers these costs while maintaining profitability.

**6. Channels and Distribution:** Define how you will reach your customers. This involves selecting appropriate distribution channels, whether it's through online platforms, physical stores, partnerships, or other means.

**7. Key Activities and Resources:** Identify the key activities your business needs to perform and the resources required to execute those activities. This could include infrastructure, technology, human resources, etc.

**8. Partnerships and Key Relationships:** Consider partnerships or alliances that can benefit your business. Whether it's suppliers, collaborators, or strategic alliances, these relationships can add value and support growth.

**9. Scalability and Adaptability:** Design a model that can scale as your business grows and adapts to changes in the market, technology, and consumer behavior.

**10. Feedback and Iteration:** Continuously gather feedback from customers and stakeholders to improve your business model. Be willing to adapt and iterate based on market dynamics and evolving customer needs.

Remember, a successful business model is not static; it evolves with the business and the market. Flexibility, innovation, and a deep understanding of customer needs are critical elements in creating and sustaining a successful business model.

## Chapter 4

A strong brand is crucial for several reasons:

**1. Recognition and Differentiation:** A strong brand helps your business stand out in a crowded marketplace. It creates recognition among consumers, distinguishing your products or services from competitors.

**2. Trust and Credibility:** A well-established brand builds trust and credibility with customers. When people recognize and trust your brand, they are more likely to choose your offerings over others.

**3. Customer Loyalty:** Strong brands often foster loyalty among customers. When people have positive experiences with a brand, they are more likely to become repeat buyers and advocates, promoting the brand to others.

**4. Premium Pricing:** A strong brand allows you to command premium prices for your products or services. Customers are often willing to pay more for brands they trust and perceive as offering higher quality or value.

**5. Emotional Connection:** Brands that evoke positive emotions and connect with customers on a deeper level tend to create stronger relationships. Emotional connections can lead to long-term customer loyalty.

**6. Consistency and Reliability:** A strong brand maintains consistency in its messaging, quality, and customer experience. Consistency builds confidence in the brand's reliability and fosters a positive perception among consumers.

**7. Attracting Talent and Partnerships:** A reputable brand attracts top talent and potential business partners. Companies with strong brands often find it easier to recruit skilled employees and establish beneficial partnerships.

**8. Resilience in Market Changes:** During market fluctuations or tough times, a strong brand tends to be more resilient. Customers may remain loyal to established brands even when faced with new options or economic challenges.

**9. Brand Extensions and Diversification:** A strong brand can successfully extend its presence into new product lines or markets. Consumers are more willing to try new offerings from a brand they already trust.

**10. Competitive Advantage:** In competitive industries, a strong brand serves as a powerful competitive advantage. It helps your business maintain and grow its market share amidst competition.

Investing in building and maintaining a strong brand is essential for long-term success. It requires consistent messaging, delivering on promises, understanding customer needs, and constantly adapting to changes in the market to stay relevant and competitive.

**Chapter 5**

Effective leadership skills are crucial for achieving business success. Here are some key leadership skills that contribute to business success:

**1. Vision and Strategic Thinking:** Effective leaders have a clear vision for the future of the business and can develop strategies to achieve that vision. They set goals, define priorities, and create a roadmap for the organization.

**2. Communication:** Strong communication skills are essential for leaders to articulate their vision, convey expectations, and inspire and motivate their teams. Listening actively and providing constructive feedback are also crucial aspects of effective communication.

**3. Decision-Making:** Leaders must make timely and informed decisions. They weigh available information, consider various perspectives, and make decisions that align with the organization's goals and values.

**4. Emotional Intelligence:** Leaders with high emotional intelligence understand their emotions and those of others. They can manage their emotions effectively, build strong relationships, empathize with their team members, and handle conflicts and difficult situations with tact.

**5. Adaptability and Flexibility:** In a dynamic business environment, leaders need to adapt to change, be open to new ideas, and be flexible in their approaches to problem-solving and decision-making.

**6. Team Building and Collaboration:** Leaders build cohesive teams by fostering a positive work culture, promoting collaboration, and leveraging the strengths of individual team members. They empower their teams, delegate effectively, and encourage a culture of trust and respect.

**7. Strategic Delegation:** Delegating tasks and responsibilities is essential for effective leadership. Delegation allows leaders to focus on high-priority tasks while empowering team members to take ownership and develop their skills.

**8. Innovation and Creativity:** Encouraging innovation and creativity within the organization fosters growth and competitiveness. Leaders should create an environment that encourages experimentation and values new ideas.

**9. Conflict Resolution:** Effective leaders are adept at resolving conflicts and managing disagreements within teams. They address conflicts constructively, promoting open dialogue and finding mutually beneficial solutions.

**10. Resilience and Problem-Solving:** Leaders need to be resilient in the face of challenges and setbacks. They approach problems with a solution-oriented mindset, finding opportunities within difficulties and guiding their teams through adversity.

Developing these leadership skills takes time and practice. Continuous self-improvement, seeking feedback, and learning from experiences are essential for leaders to enhance their capabilities and drive business success.

**Chapter 6**

Creating a great customer experience is crucial for businesses to build loyalty, satisfaction, and long-term relationships with their customers. Here are some strategies to create a memorable and positive customer experience:

**1. Understand Customer Needs:** Start by understanding your customers' needs, preferences, and pain points. Conduct market research, gather feedback, and use data analytics to gain insights into what your customers want.

**2. Provide Excellent Customer Service:**
Offer prompt, friendly, and personalized customer service across all touchpoints. Train your staff to be knowledgeable, courteous, and responsive to customer inquiries or concerns.

**3. Consistency Across Channels:** Ensure consistency in the customer experience across all channels, whether it's in-person interactions, online platforms, social media, or customer support. Maintain a cohesive brand image and messaging.

**4. Personalization:** Tailor your products, services, and communications to meet individual customer preferences. Use customer data to personalize recommendations, offers, and interactions, showing that you understand and value their needs.

**5. Simplify Processes:** Make it easy for customers to interact with your business. Simplify the purchasing process, website navigation, and product/service usage. Eliminate unnecessary steps or complexities that may cause frustration.

**6. Gather and Act on Feedback:** Encourage customers to provide feedback and listen to their suggestions or concerns. Actively use this feedback to improve products, services, and the overall customer experience.

**7. Create Emotional Connections:** Focus on creating positive emotions and memorable experiences for customers. A personalized approach, gestures of appreciation, or unexpected perks can leave a lasting impression.

**8. Empower Employees:** Empower your employees to make decisions and take actions that prioritize the customer's best interests. Encourage a customer-centric culture where employees are motivated to go above and beyond to assist customers.

**9. Transparency and Honesty:** Be transparent in your communication and dealings with customers. Build trust by being honest about your products, services, pricing, and policies.

**10. Resolve Issues Effectively:** Handle customer complaints or issues promptly and efficiently. Turn negative experiences into positive ones by addressing concerns with empathy and finding appropriate solutions.

**11. Measure and Improve:** Continuously measure customer satisfaction and gather metrics to understand the effectiveness of your customer experience efforts. Use this data to identify areas for improvement and make necessary changes.

By focusing on these strategies and consistently delivering exceptional customer experiences, businesses can build a loyal customer base and gain a competitive advantage in the market.

**Chapter 7**

Here are some effective marketing strategies tailored for small businesses:

**1. Define Your Target Audience:**
Understand your ideal customer demographics, behaviors, and needs. Tailor your marketing efforts to reach and resonate with this specific audience.

**2. Create a Strong Online Presence:**
Develop a professional website that is user-friendly, mobile-responsive, and showcases your products or services. Establish a presence on relevant social media platforms where your audience spends time.

**3. Content Marketing:** Produce valuable and relevant content that educates, entertains, or solves problems for your target audience. This can include blog posts, videos, infographics, or podcasts that showcase your expertise and build credibility.

**4. Local SEO:** Optimize your website for local search by listing your business on online directories, optimizing for local keywords, and encouraging customer reviews. This helps increase visibility in local searches.

**5. Utilize Email Marketing:** Build an email list of interested customers or prospects and send regular newsletters, promotions, updates, or valuable content. Personalize emails to enhance engagement.

**6. Leverage Social Media:** Engage with your audience on social media platforms by sharing engaging content, responding to comments, and running targeted ad campaigns to reach potential customers.

**7. Networking and Partnerships:** Establish relationships with other local businesses, industry influencers, or complementary service providers. Collaborate on events, promotions, or cross-promotional campaigns to expand your reach.

**8. Offer Promotions or Special Offers:** Use limited-time discounts, coupons, or exclusive deals to attract new customers and encourage repeat business. Highlight these offers through various marketing channels.

**9. Customer Referral Program:** Encourage satisfied customers to refer others by offering incentives, discounts, or rewards for successful referrals. Word-of-mouth referrals can be powerful for small businesses.

**10. Attend Local Events or Trade Shows:** Participate in local events, trade shows, or community gatherings to showcase your products/services, network with potential customers, and build brand awareness.

**11. Monitor and Analyze Results:** Track the performance of your marketing efforts using analytics tools. Monitor key metrics to understand what's working and what needs adjustments. Use this data to refine your strategies.

**12. Provide Excellent Customer Service:** Exceptional customer service can be a powerful marketing tool. Positive experiences can lead to word-of-mouth referrals and repeat business.

By utilizing these marketing strategies and adapting them to your specific business needs, small businesses can effectively reach their target audience, increase visibility, and build a strong brand presence within their market.

## Chapter 8

Managing finances effectively is critical for the success and sustainability of small businesses. Here's a guide on financing and managing finances for small businesses:

### 1. Create a Detailed Business Budget:

Develop a comprehensive budget that outlines your projected income, expenses, and anticipated cash flow. Include both fixed and variable costs to accurately forecast financial needs.

**2. Separate Personal and Business Finances:** Open a business bank account and keep personal and business finances separate. This simplifies accounting, taxes, and ensures proper financial management.

**3. Understand and Monitor Cash Flow:** Regularly monitor cash flow to track money coming in and going out of the business. Maintain a positive cash flow to cover operational expenses, investments, and unforeseen costs.

**4. Manage Accounts Receivable and Payable:** Stay on top of accounts receivable by promptly invoicing customers and following up on late payments. Negotiate favorable payment terms with suppliers and manage accounts payable effectively.

**5. Explore Financing Options:** Understand various financing options available for small businesses, such as business loans, lines of credit, grants, or crowdfunding. Choose the option that aligns with your needs and repayment capabilities.

**6. Control Costs:** Monitor expenses closely and look for ways to cut unnecessary costs without compromising quality. Negotiate better deals with suppliers, explore cost-effective alternatives, and optimize operational efficiency.

**7. Maintain Accurate Financial Records:** Keep meticulous financial records, including income statements, balance sheets, and cash flow statements. Use accounting software or hire an accountant/bookkeeper to ensure accuracy.

**8. Plan for Taxes:** Understand tax obligations for your business and plan accordingly. Set aside funds for taxes and take advantage of available deductions or credits to minimize tax liabilities.

**9. Forecast and Plan for Growth:** Develop financial forecasts and projections to plan for future growth and expansion. Consider how investments in marketing, technology, or personnel can contribute to business growth.

**10. Seek Professional Advice:** Consider seeking advice from financial advisors, accountants, or business consultants who can provide guidance on financial matters, tax planning, and strategic financial management.

**11. Regularly Review and Adjust:** Regularly review your financial performance against your budget and goals. Make adjustments as needed based on changes in the market, business conditions, or unexpected events.

**12. Build a Financial Cushion:** Maintain an emergency fund or reserve to cushion against unforeseen expenses or economic downturns. This helps mitigate financial risks and ensures business continuity.

By implementing these strategies and staying proactive in financial management, small businesses can maintain financial stability, make informed decisions, and position themselves for long-term success.

**Conclusion**

In the pursuit of building a thriving business, success lies in a multifaceted approach encompassing several key secrets. Effective strategies in understanding and catering to customer needs, establishing a strong brand identity, fostering innovation, cultivating a customer-centric culture, and adapting to market dynamics all play pivotal roles. However, the ultimate secret to a thriving business rests in the commitment to continuous improvement, the ability to evolve, innovate, and adapt to changing landscapes while remaining true to core values. Embracing these principles empowers businesses to not only thrive but also to leave an indelible mark in their industry, fostering sustained growth and enduring success.